This Little Explore The World book belongs to:

_____

For
Curious Learners

Published by Grant Publishing

Sales and Enquires:
grantpublishingltd@gmail.com

FOLLOW US ON SOCIAL MEDIA:
Instagram - @grantpublishingltd

GRANT
PUBLISHING

100 FACTS ABOUT SOUTH AFRICA

CONTENTS

CONTINENT

CONTINENT

A continent is a large continuous mass of land conventionally regarded as a collective region. There are seven continents: Asia, Africa, North America, South America, Antarctica, Europe, and Australia

1. South Africa is located in the continent of Africa.

2. South Africa is the southernmost country on the African continent.

CONTINENT

3. South Africa is officially called The Republic of South Africa.

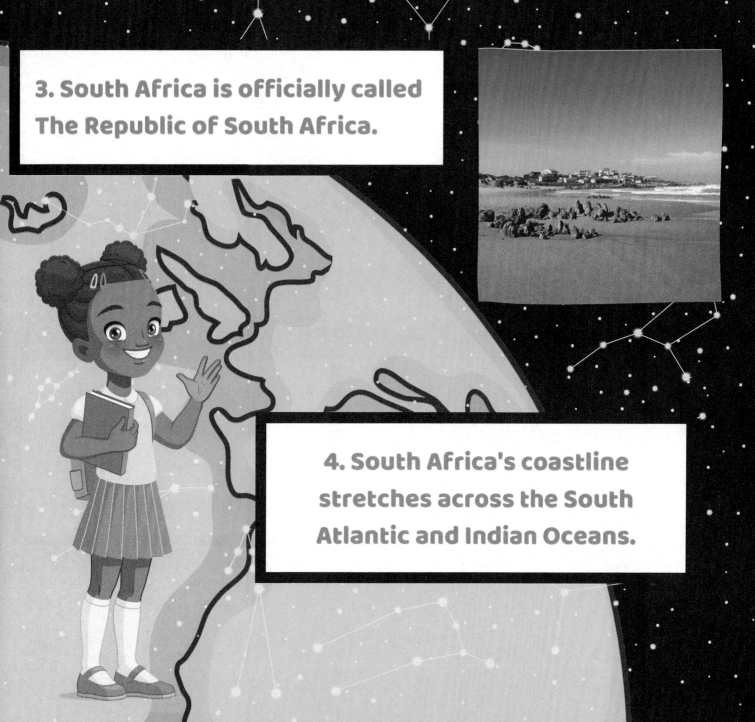

4. South Africa's coastline stretches across the South Atlantic and Indian Oceans.

5. South Africa is Africa's 9th largest country by size.

6. South Africa borders Namibia, Botswana, Zimbabwe, Mozambique and Eswatini.

ABOUT THE COUNTRY

ABOUT THE COUNTRY

A country is a distinct part of the world, such as a state, nation, or other political entity. It may be a sovereign state or make up one part of a larger state.

7. South Africa surrounds the enclaved country of Lesotho.

8. South Africa is the 23rd most populous nation in the world.

ABOUT THE COUNTRY

9. South Africa is 1,221,037 square kilometres.

10. South Africa has three capital cities.

11. South Africa has a population of over 60 million people.

12. South Africa is the southernmost country on the mainland of the Old World.

Picture of Cape Town harbour

14

13. Due to its colorful mix of cultures, South Africa is nicknamed the "rainbow nation".

14. South Africa has the highest population of all countries located entirely south of the equator.

15. The administrative capital of South Africa is Pretoria.

16. The legislative capital of South Africa is Cape Town.

Picture of Fort Bloemfontein

17. The judicial capital of South Africa is Bloemfontein.

18. The motto of South Africa is "!ke e: |xarra ‖ke".

19. The largest city in South Africa is Johannesburg.

20. In South Africa, people drive on the left side of the road.

21. The currency used in South Africa is The South African rand.

22. South Africa is a member of the British commonwealth.

LANGUAGE

Language

The Official language of a country is one designated as having a unique legal status in the state. The Regional language is one designated as having official status limited to a specific area, administrative division, or territory of the state. The National language is one that uniquely represents the national identity of a country.

23. There are 11 official languages of South Africa.

24. South Africa has the fourth-highest number of official languages in the world.

Language

25. While South Africa has 11 official languages, some are more widely spoken than others.

26. The official languages of South Africa are Zulu, Xhosa, Afrikaans, English, Pedi, Tswana, Southern Sotho, Tsonga, Swazi, Venda, and Southern Ndebele.

Language

27. Zulu is the most widely spoken and understood language in South Africa.

28. There are also many unofficial languages recognised in South Africa such as Fanagalo, Khoe, Lobedu, Nama, Northern Ndebele, Phuthi, and South African Sign Language.

RELIGION

Religion

Religion is a set of organized beliefs, practices, and systems that most often relate to the belief and worship of a controlling force.

> **29. South Africa is a religiously diverse country.**

Picture of Montagu Church in Western Cape

> **30. Christianity is the largest religions in South Africa.**

Religion

31. It is estimated that around 80 per cent of the population are Christian.

Picture of Riversdale Church in Western Cape

32. The majority of South African Christians are members of Protestant denominations.

Religion

33. Roughly 1.5 per cent of the population are Muslim.

34. About 1.2 per cent of the population are Hindu.

Religion

35. There are many sangoma living in South Africa, they are traditional healers. It is believed that around 60 per cent of people in South Africa consult with these healers.

36. There is a substantial Jewish population in South Africa.

Religion

37. South Africa's Jewish population is the 12th largest in the world.

38. About 15 percent of the population have no religious affiliation.

MUSIC

Music

Music is an arrangement of sounds having melody, rhythm, and usually harmony.

39. South Africa music has gained popularity all around the world.

Music

40. Popular music genres enjoyed by South Africans and now globally include Kwaito, Kwela, Mbaqanga, South African house, Isicathamiya, Mbube and Amapiano.

41. Popular South African musicians include Hugh Masekela, Abdullah Ibrahim, Miriam Makeba, Dave Matthews, Lucky Dube and Master KG.

PEOPLE

People

The population of a country or area is all the people who live in it.

42. South Africa is a diverse nation with multiple cultures, languages, and religions.

43. Around 80% of South Africa's population are Black South Africans.

People

44. Minority ethnicity groups in South Africa include white, Mixed raced and Asian.

45. Zulu and Xhosa are the two most spoken languages in the country.

People

46. People from South Africa are called South African.

47. Around 22 per cent of the population use Zulu as their first language.

People

48. Although Black South Africans make up most of the population, the vast majority of Black South Africans were not enfranchised until 1994.

49. South Africa houses roughly five million illegal immigrants, which includes almost three million Zimbabweans.

GEOGRAPHY

Geography

The geography of a country when you look at places within the country and the relationships between people and their environments.

50. South Africa has a temperate climate.

51. South Africa's coastline stretches more than 2,500 km.

Geography

52. South Africa is the 24th-largest country in the world.

Picture of Orange River

53. The largest river in South Africa is Orange River.

Geography

54. The highest peak in South Africa is Mafadi in the Drakensberg.

Picture of Drakensberg Mountains

55. Lake Sibaya is South Africa's largest natural freshwater lake.

Geography

56. South Africa is a land of diverse ecosystems, including deserts, plains, swamps, mountains, and jungles.

57. Climate change in South Africa has led to increased temperatures and rainfall variability.

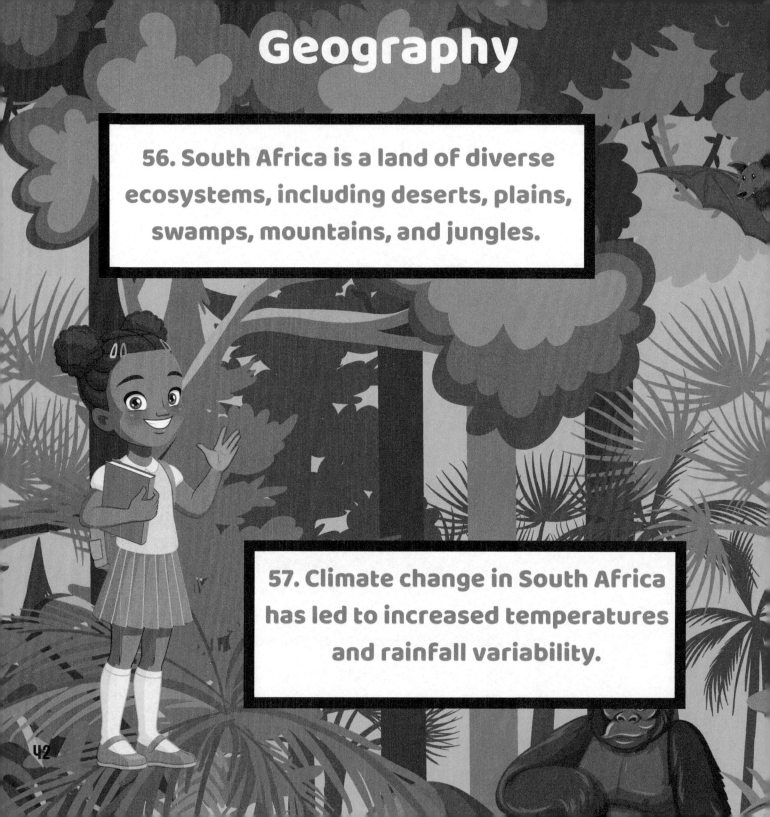

ANIMALS

Animals

An animal is any member of the kingdom of living things (as earthworms, crabs, birds, and people) that differ from plants typically in being able to move about.

58. South Africa has one of the richest biodiversity hotspots in all of Africa

59. The national animal of South Africa is the springbok.

44

Animals

60. The national bird of South Africa is the Blue Crane.

61. South Africa is home to a large variety of mammals, which includes rodents, moles, cheetahs, giraffes, shrews, bats, lions, elephants, zebras and antelopes.

FOOD

Food

A nations food describes culinary dishes that is strongly associated with a particular country.

62. South African cuisine is rich, vibrant and diverse representing the various community that inhibit the nation.

Picture of South African sausage spiral boerewors

63. South African dishes have African, Dutch, French and Malay influences.

Food

64. Boeber is a traditional South African beverage made with sugar, milk, vermicelli, sago, and flavorings such as cinnamon, rose water, star anise, and cardamom.

65. Curried dishes are popular in South Africa.

Food

66. Tropical fruits such as pineapple, coconut, banana, and mango grow in South Africa.

67. Chakalaka and pap are South Africa staple foods.

Food

68. Bobotie is considered to be the national dish of South Africa.

Picture of bobotie

69. Popular dishes in South Africa are Braai, Vetkoek, Boerewors, Bobotie, Potjiekos and Tomato Bredie.

CUSTOMS AND TRADITIONS

Customs and Traditions

A custom is a commonly accepted manner of behaving or doing something in a particular society, place or time. A tradition is the transmission of customs or beliefs from generation to generation.

70. In Xhosa culture it is popular for a person to wear complex dressing that represents their social and relationship status.

71. In South Africa it is considered polite to receive items with both hands together, held out as a cup.

Customs and Traditions

72. It is common practice to show heightened respect to elders in South Africa.

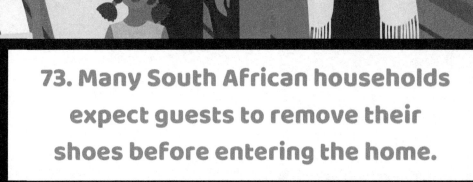

73. Many South African households expect guests to remove their shoes before entering the home.

Customs and Traditions

74. Some South African homes follow a hierarchical sequence when serving food. The order will go as follows; guests first, followed by the eldest male, remaining men, children and, lastly, women.

75. Many South Africans use the word "sorry" instead of "excuse me". For example, when asking to pass by someone who is blocking your way, South Africans may say sorry.

76. Many South Africans see it as a sign of disrespect to greet, eat, hand over, or collect things from people with your left hand.

77. 'Is it' is a popular phrase used by many South Africans when they are told a fact.

SPORTS

Sports

A sport is an activity involving physical exertion and skill in which an individual or a team competes against another or others for entertainment.

78. The most popular sports in South Africa are cricket, rugby and soccer.

79. The South African national rugby team is called the Springboks.

Sports

80. Athletics, basketball, boxing, golf, netball, swimming, and tennis are also popular in South Africa.

81. South Africa hosted the 2010 FIFA World Cup.

MONUMENTS AND ATTRACTIONS

Monuments and Attractions

A monument is a statue, building, or other structure erected to commemorate a notable person or event.

82. Robben Island is one of the most iconic monuments in South Africa. Robben Island is where former president and freedom fighting stalwart Nelson Rohihlahla Mandela was imprisoned for 27 years after attempting to overthrow the then Apartheid government.

83. South Africa is known for its golden savannah, great gaping gorges, and hauntingly beautiful deserts. Some popular attractions are Kruger National Park, The Drakensberg and Pilanesberg National Park.

CITIES

Cities

A city is a place where many people live, with many houses, stores, businesses

84. Major cities in South Africa are Cape Town, Durban, Johannesburg and Soweto.

85. Johannesburg is the most populated city in South Africa.

WELCOME
TO
DK
SOWETO

Cities

86. Cape Town is South Africa's oldest city and is often referred to as the 'mother city'.

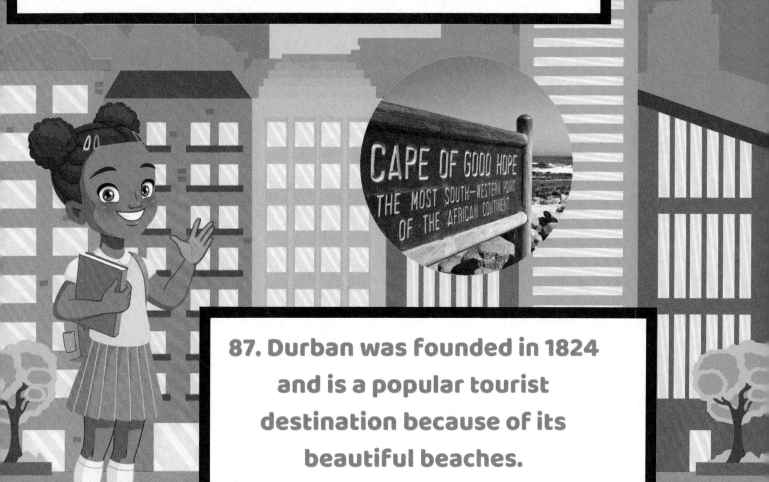

CAPE OF GOOD HOPE
THE MOST SOUTH-WESTERN POINT
OF THE AFRICAN CONTINENT

87. Durban was founded in 1824 and is a popular tourist destination because of its beautiful beaches.

HISTORY

History

History is the study and the documentation of the past.

88. Some of the earliest human fossils were discovered in Sterkfontein, a cave near the city of Johannesburg.

89. In 1652, the Netherlands established the southern city of Cape Town, and Boers (Dutch farmers), settled in the areas around the city.

History

90. In 1963, Nelson Mandela, who was the head of the anti-apartheid African National Congress, was sentenced to life imprisonment for "terrorist" activities.

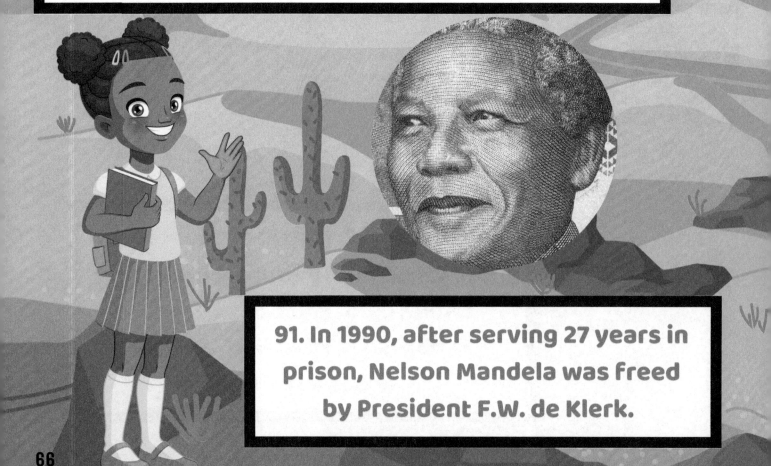

91. In 1990, after serving 27 years in prison, Nelson Mandela was freed by President F.W. de Klerk.

History

92. In 1910, the British put laws in place that separated whites from black South Africans, a practice of segregation called apartheid.

93. The South African flag was adopted on 27 April 1994.

History

94. The South African flag is a horizontally oriented Y-shape (known in heraldry as a pall) in green, with yellow (gold) and white borders, separating sections of red and blue and a black hoist triangle.

95. South Africa is nicknamed the "Cradle of Humankind."

History

96. Around 24,000 years ago, tribes of hunter-gatherers known as the San moved into South Africa.

97. Nelson Mandela was elected president of South Africa in 1994 and served until 1999.

History

98. South Africa is now the only country in the world to have hosted the Soccer, Cricket and Rugby World Cup!

99. Early dinosaur fossils have been discovered in South Africa.

History

100. The world's first heart transplant was completed in Cape Town, South Africa.

WHAT WAS YOUR FAVOURITE FACT?

WORDS FROM THE AUTHOR

"A celebration of all things Africa."

This book is an invitation to embark on a journey through time and across borders. To understand, embrace and celebrate nations that have been underrepresented in literary spheres.

Representation matters! The books we read deeply influence our understanding of who we are and what we can be. The premise of this book is to provide a small snapshot of the infinite amount of beauty in Africa lands.

If you enjoyed this book, check out our range of 100 fact books!

GLOSSARY

Currency

Currency is the official money of a country.

Ethnic group

An ethnic group is a social group or category of the population that is set apart from other groups in a society.

Ethnic minority

people who belong to an ethnic group that is a relatively small part of a population.

Independence

Not being controlled or ruled by another

Printed in Great Britain
by Amazon

58315921R00044